WILDFLOWERS

Designs for Appliqué & Quilting

CAROL ARMSTRONG

C&T PUBLISHING

Editor: Annie Nelson
Technical Editor: Diana Roberts
Copy Editor: Judith M. Moretz
Book Design: Ewa Gavrielov © 1997 C&T Publishing
Cover Production: John M. Cram and Kathy Lee
Computer Illustrations: Jay Richards © 1997 C&T Publishing
Watercolor Illustrations © 1997 Carol Armstrong
All photography by Sharon Risedorph except author photo by Carol A. Foley
Cover photo: Detail of *Pastel Garden*; © C&T Publishing

Library of Congress Cataloging-in-Publication Data

Armstrong, Carol
   Wildflowers: designs for appliqué & quilting / Carol Armstrong.
       p.   cm.
   Includes index.
    ISBN 1-57120-045-2
1. Appliqué--Patterns. 2. Quilting--Patterns. 3. Wild flowers in art.
I. Title.
TT779.A76   1998   97-39822
746.46´041--dc21   CIP

Richard Hemming & Son is a registered trademark of Entaco Limited.
Verithin is a trademark of Sanford Berol.
Poly-Fil and Soft Touch are registered trademarks of Fairfield Processing Corporation.

Published by C&T Publishing, Inc.
P.O. Box 1456
Lafayette, CA 94549

Printed in Hong Kong
10   9   8   7   6   5   4   3   2   1

TABLE OF CONTENTS

36½″ x 25″   *Bright Garden*

Dedication
To my mother, Ruth Armstrong, who is a
constant inspiration. And in memory of
my father, John Armstrong, who taught his
little girl to fish.

INTRODUCTION

I love wildflowers, and what better way to enjoy them throughout the year than appliquéd and quilted in favorite fabrics and colors? My intention with *Wildflowers: Designs for Appliqué & Quilting* is to show you easy techniques for hand appliqué of twenty-four beautiful wildflowers, as well as to offer suggestions on designing your own appliqué gardens, bouquets, and wreaths.

My style of hand appliqué abandons templates and freezer paper, utilizing a light box instead. I will show you how to appliqué flowers that accept little imperfections, mimicking the effects of the wind blowing on a petal or a bug eating the end off a leaf. When you fill your quilts with nature's bounty and beauty, minor flaws will go unnoticed.

I will teach you how to fill your backgrounds with relatively mark-free random quilt designs that tell the story of rain or wind, the falling leaves, or the buzzing trails of bees. A random design is just that—a design with no particular order. Or a scattering of pebbles with no two the same size or shape, and no repeated order in their placement. Observe nature's placement of stones in a stream bed, the branches on a tree, or the leaves on the ground after a rain storm. These are random inspirations—use them to accent your appliqué with rich and exciting patterns of lines and shadows. Delight in surprise as you experiment with random quilting as your needle draws for you.

If you are new to appliqué, welcome to hand stitching and quilting. The informal techniques that you will learn will soon be effortless. If you have already enjoyed appliqué, my journey into design will add to your experience. For everyone, I wish you the same fun I have when creating wildflower appliqué.

CHAPTER ONE

SUPPLIES

Following is a list of the basic tools and supplies you need for hand
appliqué and quilting. In addition there are always optional extras such
as a pretty pincushion, a handy thread caddy, or an elegant sewing bas-
ket. Quality materials make good quilts. When you invest a lot of time
in the making of a piece, you should also invest in quality materials.
Most importantly, have fun!

NEEDLES

Smaller needles make finer stitches. My needle of choice for appliqué is
a #10 milliners by Richard Hemming & Son®. The extra length gives me
more control when needle-turning the edges on small appliqué pieces.
I use a #10 sharps for quilting, but you may also want to try a between
needle, which is shorter. You will need a larger-eyed embroidery needle
for the embroidered details.

THIMBLES

A thimble is used to protect your fingers and keep them puncture-free.
I sometimes use a small leather thimble on my needle-pushing finger
when quilting. Otherwise, I like to feel the tip of the needle on the back
of the quilt and find that this helps keep my stitches even. There are
many styles of thimbles; try several and choose the one that is most comfortable for you.

CUTTING TOOLS

Good, sharp scissors are important. Have a small pair for snipping
threads and clipping curves, and a larger pair for cutting fabric. Both
sizes should cut to the tip of the blades. A rotary cutter, ruler, and
mat are very helpful for quick and accurate squaring up, and for cutting
borders and bindings.

LIGHT BOX

A light box is essential for appliquéing without templates. It makes
tracing and marking designs quick and easy. There are a lot of styles
and sizes available at art supply stores and at many quilt shops. In place
of a light box, you can use a window on a sunny day, or a glass table
with a small lamp underneath.

PINS

I like to have a number of glasshead pins on hand. (Always throw away any
pins that have burrs or nicks, as they could pull a thread in your work.)

Facing page:
Lilacs 29″ x 40″

Pins are helpful when appliquéing larger pieces or positioning a pre-appliquéd motif—they are that extra hand when you need it.

MARKING IMPLEMENTS

A good selection of marking pens and pencils is essential for appliqué and quilting. Quilt shops and art supply stores offer a wide selection of both. Always test your markers to see if the ink is easily removable. I use a white pencil for darker fabrics and a silver pencil, such as Verithin™, for other colors. The disappearing or washout pens can also be used to mark quilting lines, but test them first. I use them sparingly when I need to mark quilting lines. Never iron a marked piece; remove the marks first. The most important key to marking is always to mark lightly.

LIGHTING

Good lighting makes all hand sewing easier and more relaxing. I prefer daylight plus a lamp for appliqué, especially when working with dark colors. A good, bright light for evening sewing is a necessity.

IRON

A clean steam iron is a basic sewing aid. I iron on a padded surface (a few white towels on an ironing or pressing board work well). Set the iron on the cotton setting and use a bit of steam. Press from the back of the appliquéd piece, making sure not to hold the iron in one place for very long. Gently press the appliquéd piece flat and smooth; the padded surface will assist in keeping the appliqué smooth.

GETTING COMFORTABLE

Finding a comfortable place to sew is very important. When appliquéing, raising your knee or adding a pillow on your lap is helpful in controlling the background fabric. Using a footstool helps elevate your knee and prevents you from bending forward and tensing as you sew. You will know when you have found the position that works best for you when you have sewn for several hours and you are as relaxed as when you began.

FABRIC

I recommend using 100% cotton fabric because it is the easiest to use for appliqué: Pure cotton will happily respond to a finger-press and stay in place as you work. I use only solid colors and keep a large supply of rainbow colors on hand. The muslin I use is pre-shrunk, unbleached, and permanent press. I do not worry about the grain of the fabric unless I am cutting a bias strip. You can use the bias to ease sewing a curved edge by placing the curved line along the bias.

Pre-wash your fabrics if you plan on washing your finished piece. Always test for colorfastness by soaking the fabric in cool water until the water runs clear. If after rinsing the color continues to run, do not use that piece, as it may continue to bleed in the future. You may pre-shrink your fabrics in the dryer, but remove the pieces while they are still damp and finish drying them by pressing with an iron set on cotton.

> When appliquéing, keep your hands free of lotions and oils; your own body oil can make the needle difficult to handle. I wash my hands often with mild soap and cool water. Treat yourself to your favorite lotion when the sewing is set aside for the day.

BATTING

For most of my wallhangings I use Poly-Fil® traditional needle punched batting. It is a polyester blanket-like batting that shows dimension well, even when closely quilted. I also find Soft Touch® cotton batting fun to work with. It needles well and is nice for clothing or designs where you want a more old-fashioned look.

THREAD

The thread that you use is as important as the fabric. I quilt most often in neutral colored thread on unbleached muslin; however, you might choose to quilt with a colored thread. I use 100% cotton or cotton-wrapped polyester thread for basting, appliquéing, and quilting. For basting, a white thread is best. When appliquéing, match the color of the thread and appliqué fabric as closely as you can. The closer the match the more likely the stitches will seem to disappear. For best results, check the color match in natural light.

CHAPTER TWO

LIGHT BOX APPLIQUÉ: THE METHOD

Using a light box for appliqué simplifies the process by eliminating templates. The light box method is especially welcome with my wildflower patterns, as each piece is different from the next. The fewer steps you need to go through, the more fun you will have.

GENERAL INSTRUCTIONS FOR LIGHT BOX APPLIQUÉ

> If you are new to appliqué, start with a small project or enlarge the pattern a bit if the little pieces frustrate you at first. The most important reason to sew is to have fun.

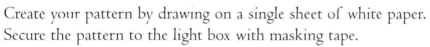

Create your pattern by drawing on a single sheet of white paper. Secure the pattern to the light box with masking tape.

Cut the background fabric about 1″ larger than needed, as it may draw up a bit during appliqué. (You can trim it to size after the appliqué is finished.) Lay the background fabric, right side up, on the light box. Using a water-soluble marker, or a silver, white, or mechanical pencil, trace the entire appliqué design onto the background fabric. Remember to mark lightly. Remove the background fabric from the light box, but leave the pattern.

Using the pattern taped to the light box, trace individual pieces onto the right side of the selected fabric with a white or silver pencil. Refer to the photos throughout the book for color ideas. Trace the exact size of each piece as it is drawn on the design. This line will be your guide for turning under. Cut out each piece ³⁄₁₆″ to ¼″ larger than the marked line. After you are comfortable with the turn-under allowance, you can cut these by eye, and the excess fabric can always be trimmed if need be. Indicate on the turn-under allowance of each piece its number for placement. This will help identify each piece, as many shapes are similar. As you learn to appliqué, mark each piece as well as the background, and always leave ample fabric to turn under. The extra fabric can always be trimmed away as necessary, and the larger initial piece is easier to work.

Opposite page:
Ruffed Grouse at Meadow's Edge
24″ x 17″

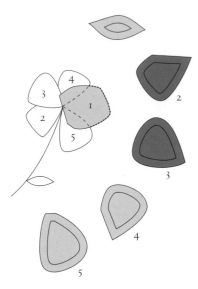

Appliqué order

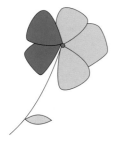

Completed Blue Flax

As you become more experienced, you may find it easier and quicker to cut the little pieces free-hand and mark the background only. This is easiest when there are not a lot of overlapping pieces that require careful placement. Often exact placement is not necessary, as in examples such as leaves, or individual petals in small flowers such as lilacs.

When appliquéing with light-colored fabrics, add a lining of the same color fabric you are using to prevent the turn-under allowance from showing through. Cut a piece the exact size of the appliqué piece with no turn-under allowance and place it behind the piece to be appliquéd. To add more dimension, you can prevent shadowing with a little piece of batting.

Begin to stitch using the numbers provided on the pattern for the order of appliqué. Pieces that will be covered by another are sewn down first. The lines on the background fabric guide the placement of each piece. Turn under the allowance to the line on the appliqué piece with the needle as you stitch, matching it with the motif marked on the background fabric. Check often that the piece is lining up. Use a pin to hold the piece in place, if needed. Turn under enough fabric for only a few stitches; do not worry ten stitches ahead. The removable nature of the markings allows a plus or minus match, so relax as you stitch. Close is good.

> Important: Only turn under and sew those edges that are exposed, not those that will be covered by another piece.

After the appliqué is finished, embroider the details such as stems, flower centers, and stamens. Remove any markings that are showing, and press the appliquéd piece from the back with an iron (set on medium), on a padded ironing surface. Trim the background to the required size.

ORDER OF APPLIQUÉ

Simply put, the pieces that are farthest away in the picture are sewn first. That is, those pieces that are covered by any others are started first. Experience will make these decisions easier. I have marked the flower patterns for the appliqué order when necessary. Unnumbered pieces can be appliquéd at any time in the sequence. When appliquéing a motif that has a number of pieces that overlap, allow yourself a little extra allowance. This will help if there is any shifting as you sew. Excess fabric can be trimmed away if everything lines up, and it is there if things do not.

APPLIQUÉD APPLIQUÉ OR PRE-APPLIQUÉ

A welcome addition to your appliqué technique, this method improves the look of many designs and makes positioning easier, especially on pre-made items. Unlike basic appliqué, where each piece is stitched to the background one at a time, the pre-appliqué technique involves stitching a partial or entire motif together before it is appliquéd to the background. Pre-appliqué creates a smoother line along the motif edges where different pieces meet.

    All of the guidelines stay basically the same. Same stitch, same marking, and most often, the same order of appliqué. Appliqué each piece to the next referring to the pattern. Do not stitch into the turn-under allowance. Leave this free for turning under when the motif is stitched in place on the background. Clip curves and trim away excess fabric as needed. Remember to change the thread color to match the color of the fabric you are stitching. Several already-threaded needles can be an added convenience, and will make the work go along quickly. When your motif is finished or a portion of a motif is ready, stitch it to the background. At times you may make several groups and then sew them together to create the entire motif. As you become more experienced with appliqué, you will naturally notice when this method is most effective.

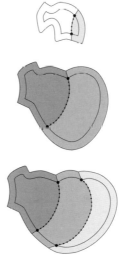

*Pre-appliqué of
Marsh Marigold leaf*   *Completed leaf*

*Pre-appliqué of
Lady's Slipper flower
and leaf*

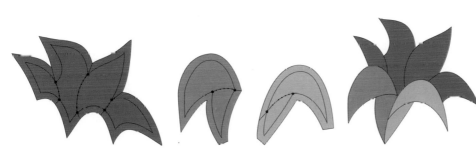

Pre-appliqué of Wood Lily petals

THE APPLIQUÉ STITCH

> Use the shaft of the needle rather than the point to
> fold the turn-under allowance. Fold and stitch, keep-
> ing in mind that the most important stitch is the one
> closest to the needle, not ten stitches ahead.

Cut, knot, and thread the needle with a 12″ to 18″ single strand of thread
in a color to match the fabric that you are appliquéing. A thread much
longer will wear out before you use it all. Using the shaft of the needle,
turn under the edge of the piece to the marked line. Slip the knot into
the fold of the turn under by running the needle through the fold from
the back of the appliqué piece and out onto the edge to be stitched down.
The knot will be hidden in the fold. It is helpful to keep the background
fabric reasonably taut when needle-turning the appliqué pieces. This
helps avoid pushing the background along with the appliqué piece as you
needle-turn. I normally have the background fabric over my knee, and the
friction of fabric on fabric is enough to hold them in place. However,
if it is a small background piece that you are working with, or if you are
appliquéing near an edge, it is helpful to pin the background down in
one spot. I pin it to my jeans or to a pillow on my lap. Since it is best to
turn the piece as you sew, you will have to re-pin as you go along. Pins
are like an extra hand and really make appliquéing much easier.

The appliqué stitch

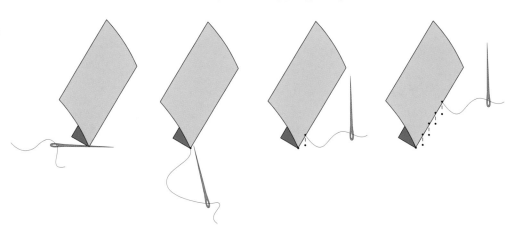

  While holding the piece to be appliquéd in the desired place on
the background, insert the needle into the background even with the
thread's exit from the appliqué piece.
  Move the needle tip forward with the needle still under the background, then come up through the background and through a few
threads on the folded edge of the appliqué piece. Pull the thread snugly
without drawing up the fabric.

Again, insert the needle into the background even with the thread's last exit from the turned edge. Travel a bit under the background and come up through the background, catching a few threads on the folded edge. (Stitches will appear directly on the fold. For an example, see page 16.) Keep folding the turn-under allowance with the shaft of the needle as you go, and trim if necessary.

Turn your work as you proceed to keep your stitching consistent and comfortable. Only worry about the stitch at hand and not what is ahead, other than an occasional check to see that the piece will line up at the end when you get there. Try to begin your appliqué at an end so that you sew the piece onto the background in one continuous line. Remember to let yourself relax and create beautiful appliqué; do not fret over little differences. Nature varies everything, and so can you.

To end, secure the thread with three stitches in the same place. If there will be another piece covering the area, you can take these stitches on the right side. Otherwise go to the back and take the stitches through the background fabric only, behind the appliqué, or tie a knot on the back if you prefer.

Being comfortable with the stitch is the key to appliqué. Practice is how to achieve this comfort. Try to keep your stitches small and evenly spaced. As you practice appliqué, your stitches will become tiny, even, and automatic.

> There is not one right way.
> The method that works for
> you is the right way.

INSIDE POINTS

Clip to the inside point just shy of the marked turn-under line. Start stitching the piece at a comfortable place that will give you a continuous line of stitching, but not at the inside point. Stitch almost to the inside point but turn under all the way to the clip.

With the needle, turn under part of the allowance, on the opposite side, down to the clip. Hold in place.

Put the needle under the appliqué and pivot, rolling the allowance under and around the point. Hold in place and stitch to the inside point. Take one or more tiny stitches at the inside point, then adjust the turn-under on the way out of the inside point, and continue around the piece.

Inside point

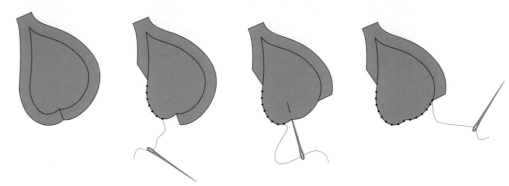

If an inside point just won't work for you, cut the piece into two pieces and pre-appliqué the two together. Mark the line splitting the inside point. Cut two pieces with turn-under allowances, then pre-appliqué along the center line. Appliqué as a single piece.

*Pre-appliqué of
inside point*

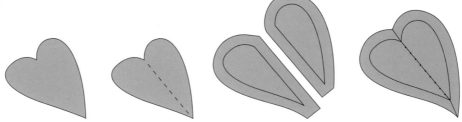

INSIDE CURVES

For inside curves, clip as many times as needed for a smooth turn-under. When curves are tight, use the same pivoting needle as used for inside points. Practice sewing tight curves and inside points on scrap fabric. When designing my flowers and birds I try to create designs which avoid difficult turn-unders wherever possible.

*Clipping inside curve;
Bloodroot leaf*

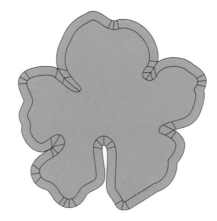

POINTS

I have found that some shapes are easier to stitch starting at the point: the point of a leaf on a stem, the point of a teardrop or heart shape, a point toward the center of a flower, or on any piece where I will begin and end at the same point. Points are not difficult once you have sewn a few. The sharper the point the slower you should work to ease the allowance under.

Square off the end of the point leaving a ³⁄₁₆″ turn-under allowance. The best rule to follow is, if it is too much to turn under, cut it off. Fold under the allowance straight across the point. Bring your thread up through the exact point, hiding the knot in the fold. Take one stitch.

Hold the end down and, using the shaft of the needle, turn under a portion of the allowance beyond the point, then stitch. Continue stitching to the next point. Make a stitch at the exact point on your appliqué shape. Take another very tiny second stitch to secure the piece. Clip the excess fabric at the point. Push the allowance under with your needle and start to stitch the second point.

You have now finished two points: one a beginning point and the other a point within a line of stitching. Not so bad, is it?

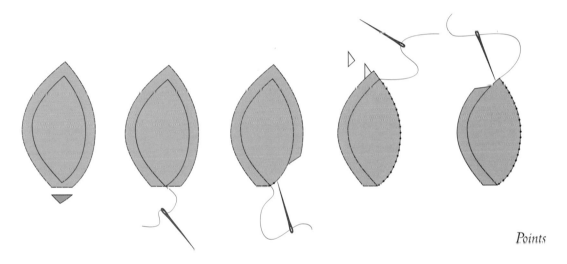

Points

BIAS STRIPS

Bias strips can be used for stems, branches, or any thin line you want to appliqué, especially if that line is curved. Bias is cut at a 45° angle to the straight grain, is not easily frayed, and has some stretch.

For stitching larger widths of bias, simply cut your bias strip the width of the finished line plus the turn-under allowance on both sides. For example, cut a bias strip ¾″ wide for a desired ¼″-wide finished stem. Finger-press the allowance along one side and stitch in place following the marking on the background. Turn the other side under with your needle as you go. On a curve, I sew inside the curve first.

For tiny bias lines, I cut the strip about ½″ wide so that it is easy to handle. As with wider strips, finger-press one side and stitch in place according to your design. Then flip the piece open to expose the turn-under allowance and carefully trim it close to the stitch line, leaving enough fabric to secure the piece. Flip the piece back and trim to the width needed plus a ³⁄₁₆″ width or less turn-under. A good rule of thumb is to trim the turn-under allowance to the width of the finished stem. Needle-turn the allowance along the other side. You will be amazed at how tiny a line you can create with just a little practice.

Regular bias stems

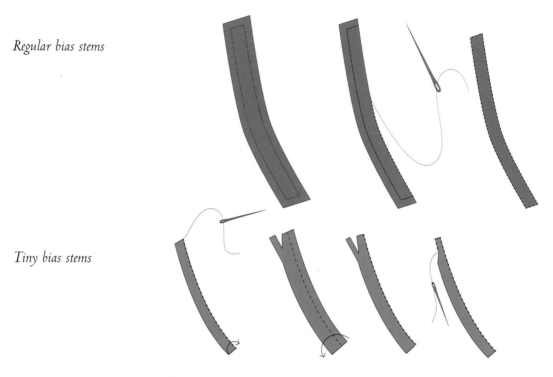

Tiny bias stems

CIRCLES

The most important aid in turning circles, both large and small, is to go one stitch at a time, and then turn. Again, take one stitch and turn. If you do end up with a little point along the curve, bring your needle out through the point and then back through the background, pulling the point inward. Use the marking on the background and the natural curvature of the piece to assist in smooth lines.

Circles

EMBROIDERY

For those details that are too tiny for appliqué, I use some simple embroidery stitches. Embroidery is the last step after the appliqué. Small adjustments can be made with embroidery if the flower you have appliquéd became a little "windblown" or "nibbled by a bug." I rarely use a hoop when embroidering these small details, but you will need a way to keep the work flat as you go. In most cases I use two strands of embroidery floss. Following are some basic stitches that will fill most needs.

FRENCH KNOT

This creates great flower centers, with one or many in a cluster. It also creates tiny heads at the end of flower stamens.

Note: You can increase the size of the knot by using more strands of floss. Bring the needle up from the wrong side of fabric. Wrap floss around the needle twice and insert the needle back into the fabric close to the thread's exit. Pull the knot tight (but not too tight) and pull the needle through, holding the knot until all the floss is pulled through.

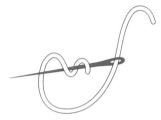

French knot

STEM STITCH

Just like it sounds, it makes thin stems, as well as any fine line such as a stamen. To make the stems thicker, stitch two or more lines next to one another.

Stem stitch

SATIN STITCH

For the slightly larger areas that need to be filled—such as a bird's eye, a larger flower center, or stamen end—use this stitch for coverage.

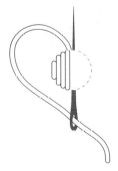

Satin stitch

CHAPTER THREE

QUILTING & FINISHING

Quilting is drawing another picture behind your appliqué "painting." It creates a marvelous pattern of shadows, light, and lines. As if you were drawing, your needle can travel as easily as a pencil. You can use quilting to represent the darting paths of bugs in a meadow, or rays of bright sunlight. You can make it rain, let the wind blow, or have a stone fall in the pond. Let quilting draw your leaves and branches, grass in the background, and flowers in the distance. The possible patterns are as endless as your imagination.

Opposite page: Sand Hill Crane 26½" x 42"

I enjoy quilting random and asymmetrical designs. I do not quilt the appliqué design. That is, when your quilt line comes up to an appliquéd piece, go underneath, between the layers, and come up on the other side. If the appliquéd area is too large to go underneath, end your quilting thread and start up on the other side.

BORDERS

Borders are the frame for the appliquéd "picture." You may add one or more in different widths. Always measure your appliquéd piece and trim to the desired size before adding borders, being sure that borders opposite each other are the same size. I stitch the side borders first and then add the top and bottom borders stitching straight across. Repeat the order if you add a second border. Use a ¼" seam allowance when sewing the borders.

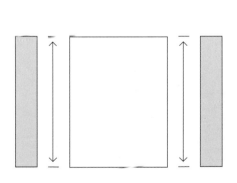

Measure and add side borders

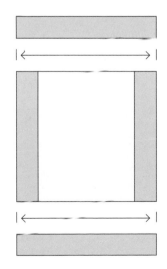

Measure and add top and bottom borders

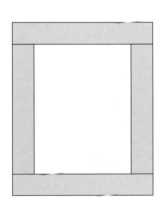

Completed borders

MARKING

There are specific ways to mark, especially when you are first starting out. The less marking you do, the less you have to remove. I use a water-soluble marker when necessary and always mark very lightly. Some designs, such as Double Wedding Ring (see page 90), need to be marked before basting. Using a light box, trace your design onto the top of the fabric. Any design that is going to repeat itself needs to be marked to keep consistency. For random designs, pre-marking is not necessary. Use a marker lightly, as if you were sketching, or even better, use the tip of your needle. Draw the needle across the fabric, pressing the tip into the fabric to create a line that will stay long enough for you to quilt the marked line. Just mark as you go. Use masking tape to mark straight lines. I press the tape onto a scrap of fabric first to de-sticky it, and then use the tape to mark lines as I stitch. If you feel the need, you can cut small shapes for templates out of stiff interfacing or some other non-raveling fabric. Simply pin the shapes to the basted top and quilt around them. For random designs, ideally you will eye your stitches as if you were doodling. I often make up my designs as I quilt, not knowing the complete picture ahead of time. One area of quilting leads to an idea for another. The more you practice the less you will need to mark.

BASTING THE LAYERS

This step is important to ensure a smooth quilt. Cut your backing and batting an inch or so larger than the top all around. On a smooth surface lay out the backing, then batting, and finally the top. Keep the layers smooth and flat. Using white thread, baste the three layers together. For my wallhangings, I baste a grid of horizontal and vertical lines four inches apart using one-inch-long stitches. I lap quilt without a frame, as this is most comfortable for me.

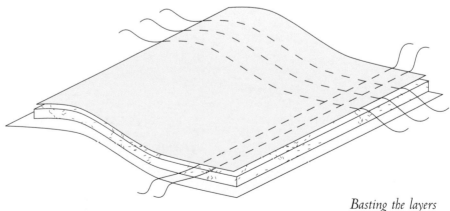

Basting the layers

THE QUILTING STITCH

I use a running stitch for quilting. Just in and out, taking several stitches on the needle each time, depending on the amount of curve in the pattern. As you quilt, do not push or pull the layers separately. Trust the basting and let the quilt relax as you stitch. Be sure to catch all three layers.

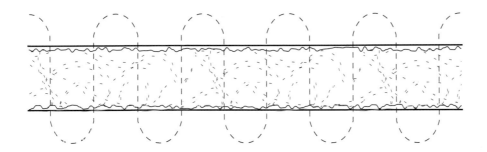

Quilting stitch

To begin, knot a 12" length of quilting thread—a length much longer will wear as you stitch. Pull the knot through the top into the batting and come up to the top again to begin. To end a thread, put a knot in the thread close to the quilt top and pull it into the batting. Let the needle travel between the layers an inch or so, then come up, and snip. This will leave a tail inside the quilt.

DESIGNS

Now that you know how to baste and quilt, you must think about the design you would like to quilt. You can begin from an appliquéd motif and work outward, see page 10; or design a separate picture independent of the appliquéd design, see page 70. Working from the center out helps keep the piece flat. Follow the center guideline as near as the design allows, but do not let that rule the design. If your basting is secure, you can begin anywhere on the piece. A little practice and you're off and running!

A design library is a great source to help you think of ideas. You can play out your thoughts on paper and doodle some designs, save the ones you like, and put them on index cards for reference. Following is a start on a design collection that I created. I am sure you will add many ideas of your own.

Quilting Designs

BINDING

Binding is the finished edge for your quilt. For square or rectangular pieces, I use a single-fold straight-grain binding. For quilts with curved edges, like the Double Wedding Ring on page 90, it is necessary to use a bias binding. All of the projects, except the Double Wedding Ring, require a ¼ yard of fabric. I cut the binding strips 2″ wide selvage to selvage using a rotary cutter, ruler, and mat. In the same order as the borders, I stitch the binding on the sides and then top and bottom. I use a ½″ seam allowance, which makes a finished binding width of ½″. Turn the binding to the back, and turning under the raw edge ½″, blind stitch it down, being careful not to let any stitches go through to the front. Miter fold the corners following the illustration. I pin the entire binding in place before stitching it down on the back. Always sign and date your finished piece.

FABRIC GRAIN

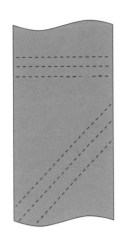

straight grain

bias grain

ADDING BINDINGS

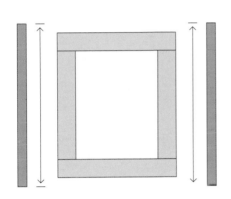

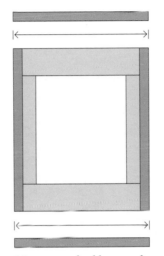

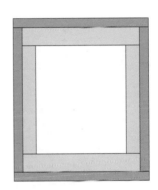

Measure and add side bindings

Measure and add top and bottom bindings

Binding ready to turn back

BINDING CORNERS

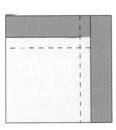

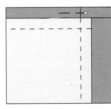

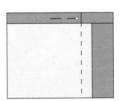

Stitch top binding strip onto quilt

Stitch side binding strip onto quilt

Fold top strip as shown

Fold again as shown

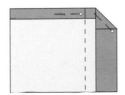

Fold side strip at 45° angle as shown

Fold as shown

Fold again as shown

Front

CHAPTER FOUR

TWENTY-FOUR
WILDFLOWERS TO APPLIQUÉ

The following wildflower patterns are numbered for the appliqué order
and include any special instructions.

BLEEDING HEART

This wildflower is a denizen of richly shaded woods, with a drooping row of pink "hearts" beneath the foliage. A relative called Dutchman's Breeches has a creamy flower with a yellow tip.

APPLIQUÉ: Follow the appliqué order.

EMBROIDERY: Stem stitch the stems with two strands of green floss.

BLOODROOT

A Bloodroot is a single, white delicate wild-flower. The petals stay but two or three days in early spring, and a breath of wind may blow them away even sooner. At the flower's center are rod-like yellow filaments. The petals can number from eight to ten, or more. The leaf grows quite large after the flower is gone. The reddish juice of the root gives this flower its name.

APPLIQUÉ: Begin with the stems if you appliqué them, or leave until last if you choose to embroider. Then appliqué the leaf, followed by the petals. The petals do not meet in the middle on the open flower, which gives the bloom a delicate look.

EMBROIDERY: Stems are stem stitched if not appliquéd. Take single, long, straight stitches with two strands of yellow floss for the stamens, which meet at the center of the open flower.

BLUE FLAG

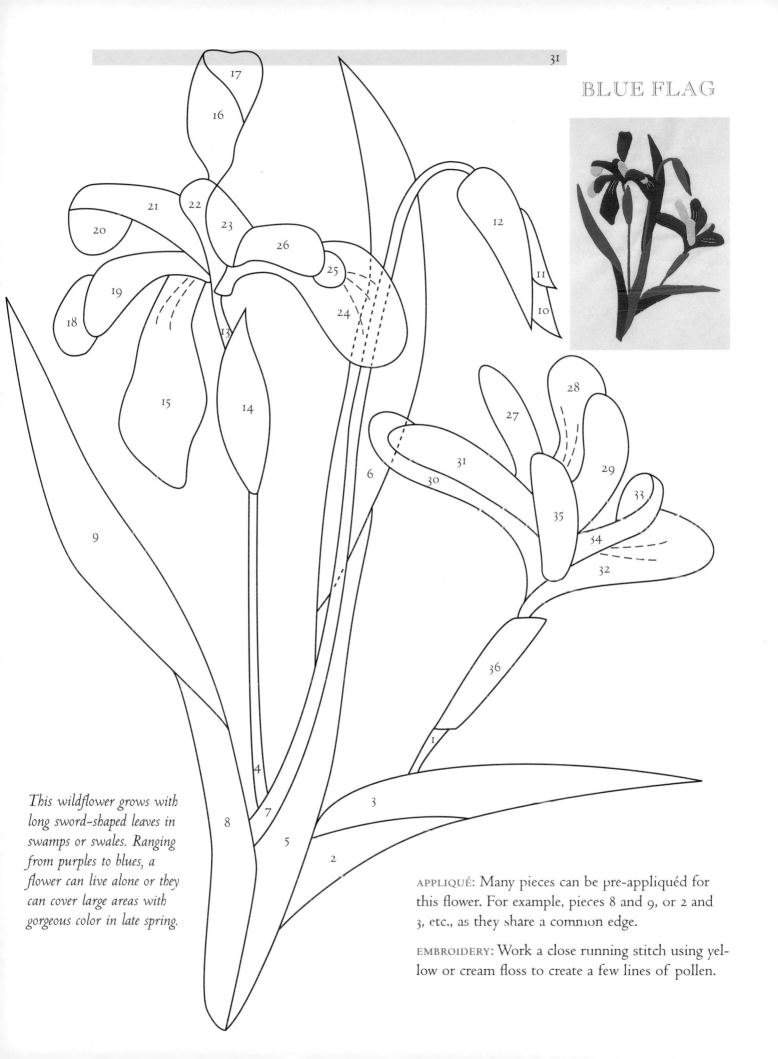

This wildflower grows with long sword-shaped leaves in swamps or swales. Ranging from purples to blues, a flower can live alone or they can cover large areas with gorgeous color in late spring.

APPLIQUÉ: Many pieces can be pre-appliquéd for this flower. For example, pieces 8 and 9, or 2 and 3, etc., as they share a common edge.

EMBROIDERY: Work a close running stitch using yellow or cream floss to create a few lines of pollen.

BLUE FLAX

A slender stem with delicate blue flowers characterizes this plant. This species' seed is cultivated for oil and its fiber for linen.

APPLIQUÉ: Follow the appliqué order. For additional help, see illustration on page 12.

EMBROIDERY: Work one or two French knots in the flower centers with black or blue floss. Stem stitch for the stems with two strands of green floss.

BUNCH BERRY

APPLIQUÉ: Sew the stems first with bias strips, or embroider later. Follow the appliqué order.

EMBROIDERY: Make an abundance of French knots for the centers, using yellow, cream, or green floss.

Also known as Dwarf Cornel; what appear to be white petals are actually modified leaves surrounding tiny greenish to cream-colored flowers in the center. The flower sits on a short stem above a whorl of six leaves. Later in the season a cluster of red berries replaces the white center.

BUTTERCUP

Glossy yellow petals numbering from five to seven are filled with bushy stamens in the center. A flower found often in wet meadows, it can grow from two to three feet tall.

APPLIQUÉ: Follow the appliqué order.

EMBROIDERY: Work straight stitches with French knots at the ends for the buttercup centers' stamens. Stem stitch the stems with two strands of green floss.

CALIFORNIA POPPY

*Beautiful, bold orange blossoms say poppy.
One of my favorites, these flowers can
cover entire hillsides in carpets of gold.*

APPLIQUÉ: Appliqué the large stems
first, or embroider later if you choose.
Follow the appliqué order.

EMBROIDERY: Use several straight
stitches or a satin stitch for the stamens.
Stem stitch the small stems and use a
double row of stem stitch if you chose
to embroider the larger stems.

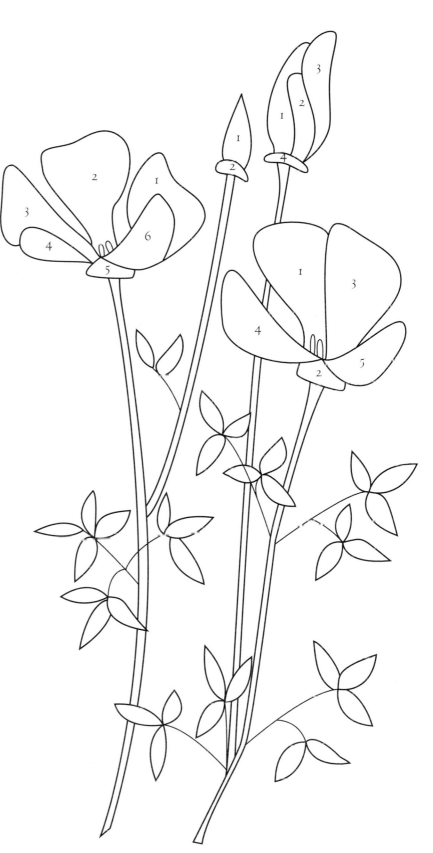

COLORADO COLUMBINE

APPLIQUÉ: Appliqué the stems first, or embroider later. Follow the appliqué order.

EMBROIDERY: Use two lines of stem stitch if you choose to embroider the stems. Work long straight stitches, using yellow floss, radiating the stamens from the flower centers.

Soft purples to lavender blues topped with bright white center petals create a wonderful bloom to appliqué. These sturdy plants find their home at high altitudes. They create an astounding splash of color in the wilderness.

FIREWEED

Blooming in summer and fall, this tall spiked flower lives in meadows and swales. The four petals of this conspicuous blossom range from pinks to purples. They have alternate willow-like leaves along a stem that is often reddish in color.

APPLIQUÉ: Follow the appliqué order.

EMBROIDERY: Stem stitch for the stems, using a double row for the main stem. A single strand of floss with a French knot at the end forms each stamen.

FRINGED GENTIAN

These very showy bright blue or violet flowers live in woods, meadows, and swales. They are composed of a tube base with four fringed petals. These relatively rare wildflowers bloom in late summer to fall. Although open in the sunshine, these blossoms close on cloudy days and at night.

APPLIQUÉ: Follow the appliqué order.

EMBROIDERY: Stem stitch for the stems with two strands of green floss.

HARE BELL

A bell-shaped nodding flower ranging from blue to pink to white, they bloom during summer in rocky and sandy places.

APPLIQUÉ: Follow the appliqué order.

EMBROIDERY: Stem stitch for the stems with two strands of green floss.

INDIAN PAINTBRUSH

This plant thrives in sandy soils and has red to orange-tipped bracts. The leaves at the base form a rosette, and leaves grow from the hairy stem. This is an early spring plant.

APPLIQUÉ: Take your time with these small pieces and remember, there is room for variance in the natural world. Follow the appliqué order.

EMBROIDERY: Stem stitch for the stems with two strands of green floss.

LADY'S SLIPPER

This impressive flower, blooming in bogs and wet meadows in early summer, is part of the orchid family. There are several other varieties of wild orchids, one among them being a very similar Yellow Lady's Slipper.

APPLIQUÉ: Some pre-appliqué is helpful. Appliqué piece 3, the little stem, onto piece 2. Then stitch piece 4 to this motif and appliqué as one piece. Pre-appliqué piece 8 to 7 as well.

EMBROIDERY: None.

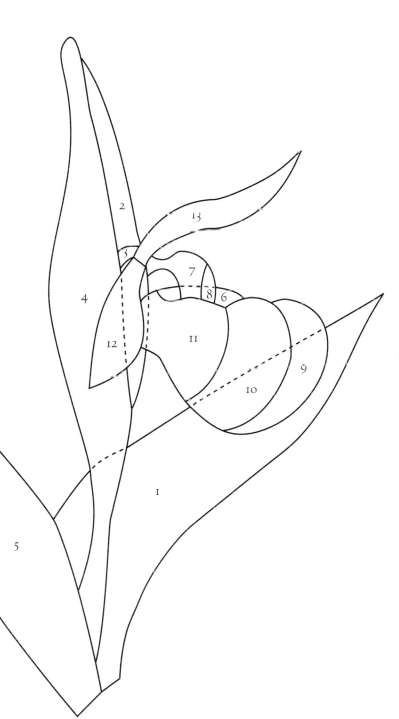

LUPINE

From blue, blue-violet, to pink, to white, these flowers grow on short stalks from a central stem. They are common to sandy places and meadows.

APPLIQUÉ: Follow the appliqué order, but exact placement is not critical. Allow yourself some freedom for design.

EMBROIDERY: Stem stitch for the stems with two strands of green floss.

MARSH MARIGOLD

This plant, which thrives in wet places, can grow even in shallow waters. The conspicuous yellow flowers have five to nine petals surrounded by large round to heart-shaped leaves. Often found growing in colonies, these groups of flowers are a welcome bright spot in early spring.

APPLIQUÉ: Appliqué the stems first using bias, or embroider later. Pre-appliqué the two leaf pieces. Note that the flower petals do not touch in the center. For additional help, see illustration on page 13.

EMBROIDERY: Use long, straight stitches ending in French knots for stamens. Have the straight stitches meet in the empty center of the flowers. Using two different colors, such as green and yellow, will give dimension. Use a double row of stem stitches for the stems if you did not appliqué them.

ORANGE HAWKWEED

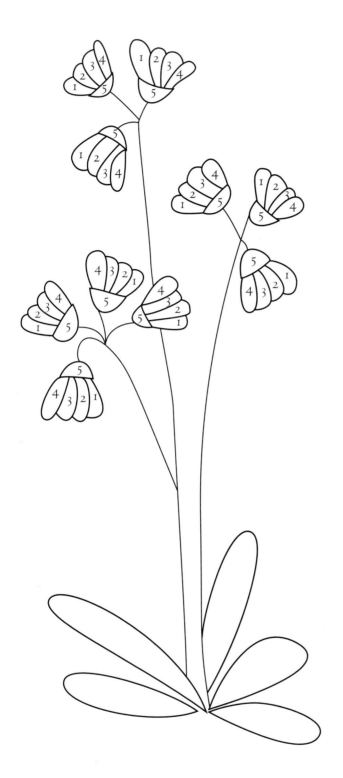

Also known as Devil's Paintbrush, these flowers can cover an entire field with a blaze of color. The flowers cluster in a group at the top of a single stem.

APPLIQUÉ: Take your time with the small pieces. Follow the appliqué order.

EMBROIDERY: Stem stitch for the stems with two strands of green floss.

OX-EYE DAISY

These bright white blossoms fill meadows in the summer. They can have as many as fifteen to twenty petals.

APPLIQUÉ: Appliqué all the petals first and then cover the unturned ends with the yellow center. There is a lot of room for variation with this flower design.

EMBROIDERY: Stem stitch for the stems with two strands of green floss.

SHOOTING STAR

There are many species of this flower, and they can have petals which vary from white to pink to purple. A yellow ring is at the top of a spear-like point, formed by the clinging dark stamens.

APPLIQUÉ: Treat the stamen point and the ring as a single piece of dark fabric. You may pre-appliqué the two leaf pieces.

EMBROIDERY: Using yellow floss, form the ring at the top of the stamens with one or two rows of stem stitches. Stem stitch for the stems with two strands of green floss.

SWAMP ROSE

A wild rose common to the edges of streams or swamps, this bush species can grow up to six feet in height. Five pink petals surround a yellow disc with numerous stamens.

APPLIQUÉ: Appliqué the larger stems, or they can also be embroidered later. Follow the appliqué order.

EMBROIDERY: With green floss, stem stitch the smaller stems, and use two rows of stem stitch for the main stem if you did not appliqué. Surround the centers with many French knots using yellow floss.

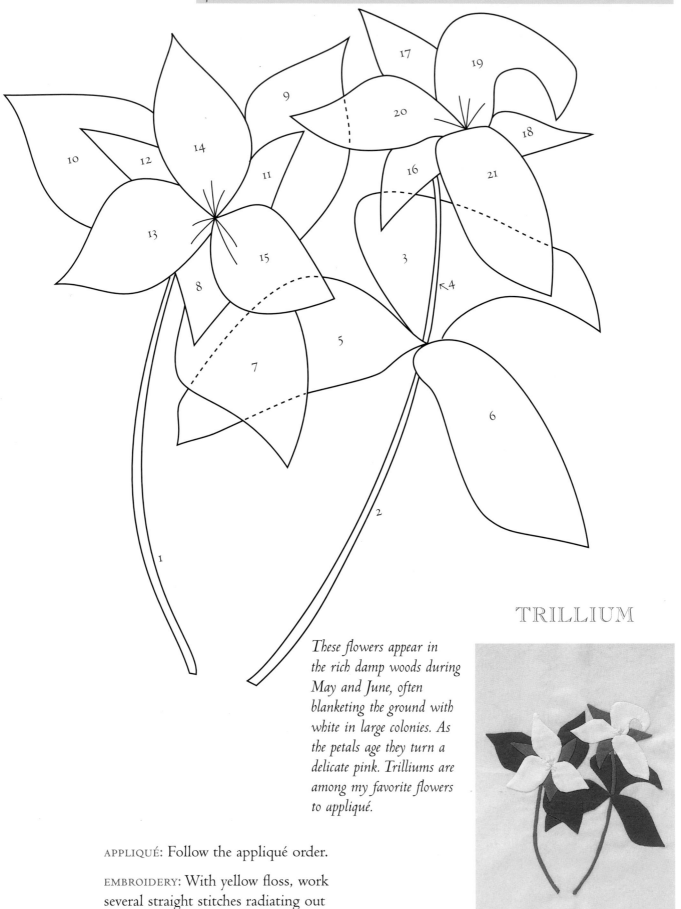

TRILLIUM

These flowers appear in the rich damp woods during May and June, often blanketing the ground with white in large colonies. As the petals age they turn a delicate pink. Trilliums are among my favorite flowers to appliqué.

APPLIQUÉ: Follow the appliqué order.

EMBROIDERY: With yellow floss, work several straight stitches radiating out from the center for the stamens.

TROUT LILY

This plant grows in colonies in the spring. Usually only a few of the two-leafed plants are blooming, with the rest being single-leafed.

APPLIQUÉ: Use bias strips for the stems, or embroider them later. Follow the appliqué order.

EMBROIDERY: Use two lines of stem stitch for the stems if not appliquéd. Stem stitch the stamens ending with a small satin stitch or a French knot for the anther.

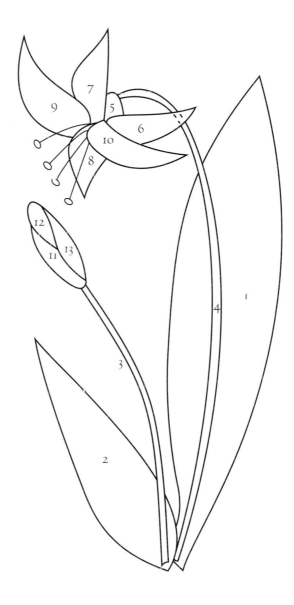

VIOLET

There are a lot of types of violets, but they all share similar heart-shaped leaves. These flowers decorate the forest's shady places with yellow, blue, purple, and white.

APPLIQUÉ: Follow the appliqué order.

EMBROIDERY: Stem stitch for the stems with two strands of green floss. Complete this flower by stitching two or three straight stitches from the center downward in a yellow floss, and adding a black floss French knot in the center.

WILD COLUMBINE

These reddish flowers with yellow centers hang from delicate stems. With leaflets of three, these April-to-June blossoms grow in rocky woodlands. Their nectar is especially attractive to butterflies and hummingbirds.

APPLIQUÉ: Follow the appliqué order.

EMBROIDERY: Stem stitch for the stems with two strands of green floss. Stem stitch, or use long stitches, for the stamens, and end each one with a French knot worked in yellow floss.

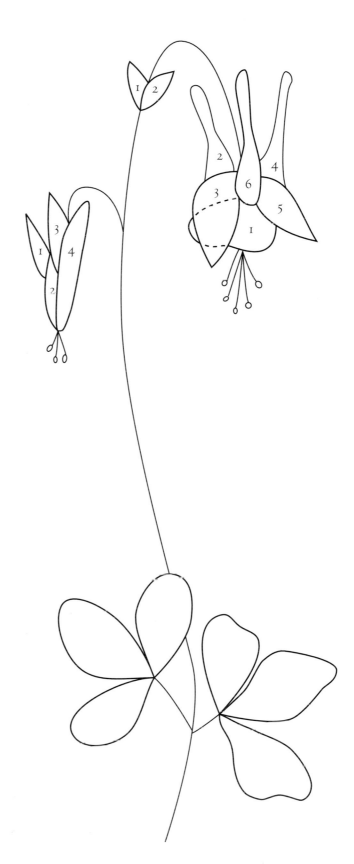

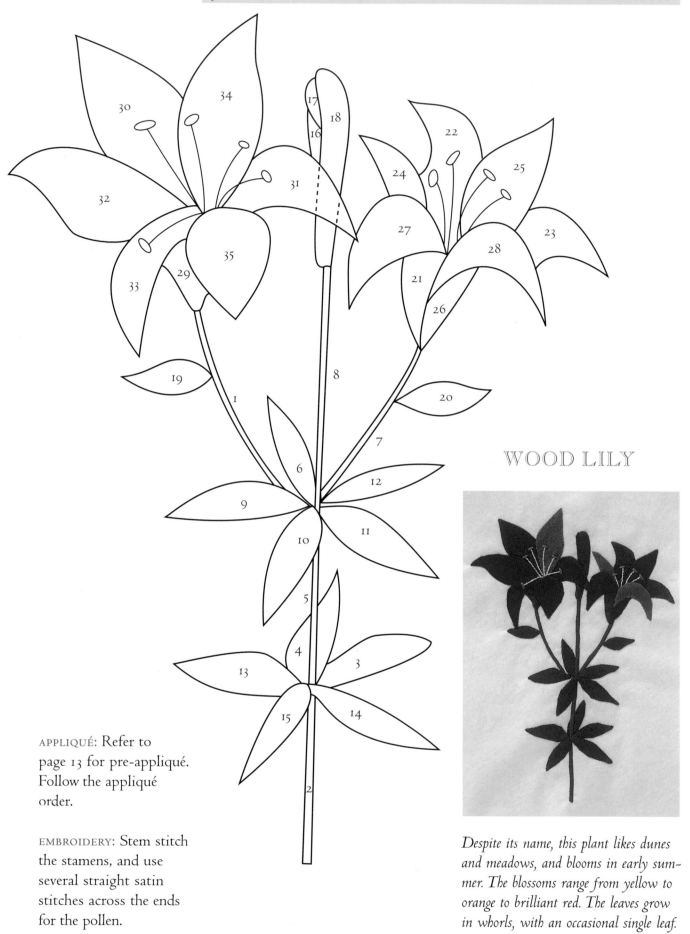

WOOD LILY

APPLIQUÉ: Refer to page 13 for pre-appliqué. Follow the appliqué order.

EMBROIDERY: Stem stitch the stamens, and use several straight satin stitches across the ends for the pollen.

Despite its name, this plant likes dunes and meadows, and blooms in early summer. The blossoms range from yellow to orange to brilliant red. The leaves grow in whorls, with an occasional single leaf.

DESIGNING
YOUR OWN PATTERNS

Designing your own wildflower garden can be fun and easy using the patterns in this book. To begin you will need a light box or tracing paper, a sharp pencil, an eraser, a fine-line black marker, some colored pencils, crayons, or watercolors, and individual flower patterns. (I find it easiest to use the patterns at one-half the size when designing.) After I have a finished design, I either redraw it using the full-size patterns or enlarge the small version at a print shop. The watercolor illustrations included in this book are all shown at one-half the size; they have been included for personal use.

First you need to decide what size image you would like to design for appliqué. It is better to begin with smaller projects and tackle larger ones as you gain more experience. Perhaps you might start with a small motif for a quilt block, or a motif to decorate fabric or a pillow. Or it could become an entire garden for the wall! I always have many more design ideas ready in my head than the time to stitch them, but that is part of the fun —deciding which project to start.

You can have a theme for your design such as: color, time of year the blossoms appear, size of the flowers, where the flowers grow, or any combination that you like. For example, if you choose the theme "time of year the blossoms appear," you could create a summer wildflower design incorporating the Buttercup (page 34), Hare Bell (page 39), Ox-Eye Daisy (page 45), and Wood Lily (page 52) for a beautiful combination. Let your designs reflect your personality.

After you have chosen a size for your design—horizontal, vertical, square, or round—it is simply a matter of tracing the flower patterns that you want to use. Keep in mind that the flowers can be easily "grown" to fit your design. Do not hesitate to reverse the flowers for a different look. Simply put them on the light box and trace the reverse images. Or "snip" off a flower head, make the stem longer, replace the blossom, and add a few extra leaves. For variety, curve the stem, as if it were blowing in the wind. You can leave some petals off, rearrange the leaves, add another flower head or bud—whatever your imagination allows. By tracing the designs, you can make variations with ease.

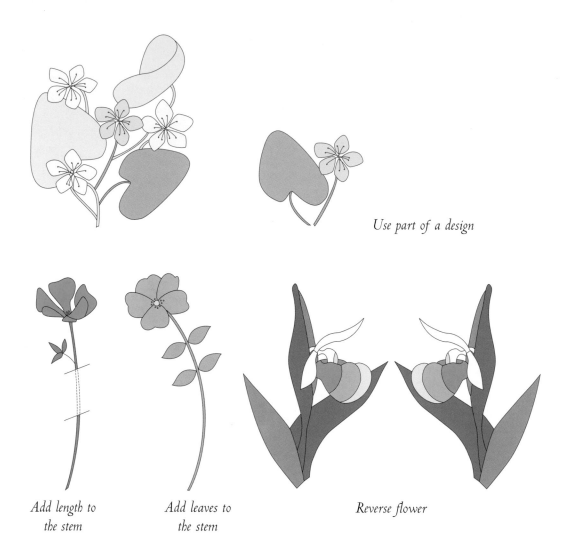

Use part of a design

*Add length to
the stem*

*Add leaves to
the stem*

Reverse flower

Begin your design by placing any flower in the front of the drawing, and
trace it entirely. Then start adding additional flowers, but do not trace
those parts that are covered by the flower in front. Continue in this
manner until you have a "painting" that pleases you. You need not overlap the flowers at all times and can line them up for a garden look. It is
all up to you.

To make a wreath, mark a circle the size you want, or use a heart,
oval, or even a square shape. The line you have drawn will be your
general guide for placing the flowers, parts of flowers, a combination of
flowers, or just a single much-loved flower. See the wreath project on
page 70 for an example.

For small appliqué motifs for items such as shirt pockets, little
gifts, ornaments, or any piece that you would like to accent, a little
flower "cutting" is in order. "Snip" a flower head, or several, of your
choice, and arrange them in a space that will work for your planned

project. Treat the drawn flowers the same as if you were arranging them in a tiny vase. The advantage is that you can "regrow" these flowers any way you like.

After designing a piece you may want to set it aside and look at it now and then for several days. Take it to a mirror. The reverse image often shows imperfections. I find that after a few days, if I still like it, the design will make a nice appliqué. On to the coloring.

Get out your colored pencils, watercolors, or crayons, choose one or more copies of the design, and start to color. If you use the smaller version of your design, you will progress more quickly. If you are unsure of the colors, make several different versions. This will give you a good idea of what the appliquéd version will look like, and you can easily refer to it while you are cutting fabric.

Now that your design is to your liking (and full size), it is ready to put on the light box. To make tracing a bit easier through the fabrics, mark the design with a black fine-line marker.

Once you begin designing patterns, you will soon find that you have dozens of wonderful ideas. These designs can be sewn onto everything from quilts to clothing to home decor items—so pick up that pencil and go, then take up the needle and sew!

CHAPTER FIVE

PROJECTS

The following projects will give you ideas for how to use the twenty-four wildflower patterns. I want to encourage you to design your own wildflower projects. To get you started I have created ten projects using the patterns in this book and some additional wildflowers and birds. These projects are meant to spark your creativity and give you new ideas.

Carol Armstrong

POPPY AND FLAX NAPKINS
AND TABLE RUNNER

Here's a simple project that will impress your guests at your next dinner party. You can make your own napkins and table runner in the fabric of your choice, or purchase them pre-made. Select colors that suit your decor; the sizes of the fabric pieces are flexible.

MATERIALS

Napkins: approximately 16″ square
Table runner: approximately 13″ wide by 36″ or more in length
Selection of fabrics for appliqué
Matching thread
White and navy blue embroidery floss for flower details

APPLIQUÉ

Appliqué all the stems first then the flowers. Follow the appliqué order. Unnumbered pieces may be added at any time. Try to keep the back neat, as it will not be hidden behind batting and backing. Embroider the details last, then remove any markings and press.

Table runner pattern

Center

Photocopy at 125% to
increase pattern to size
of the finished project

Napkin pattern

100% size

DOILY AND SACHET BAG

Appliqué motifs can adorn almost any fabric item. A few flowers can brighten up a simple white doily. Decorate a dresser top with colorful hand-appliquéd sachet bags, or give the sachets as special gifts.

DOILY MATERIALS

A doily with a fabric center approximately 4″ in diameter
Selection of fabrics for appliqué
Matching thread
Green embroidery floss for flower stems

Doily center

DOILY

This doily design is an adaptation of the Bleeding Heart pattern.
Keep the back tidy, as it will not be hidden with backing. Embroider
the details, remove the markings, and press. Starch lightly, if needed.

SACHET BAG MATERIALS

8½″ square of fabric
Selection of fabrics for appliqué
Matching thread
Dark green and red embroidery floss for stems and flower details
12″ piece of ½″- wide ribbon to tie the sachet
Polyester stuffing
A few cotton balls scented with aromatic oil (for stuffing)

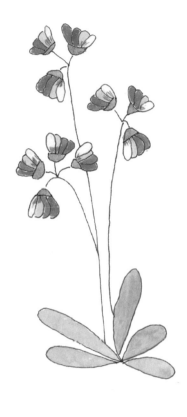

Sachet bag pattern

SACHET BAG

Mark the appliqué design on the square of fabric according to the diagram. Following the appliqué basics, appliqué the design and embroider
the details. Remove any markings, and press.

Using a ¼″ seam, machine stitch the seam in the back with right
sides together. Centering the back seam with right sides still together,
stitch across the bottom of the bag. Turn the bag right side out, and

press. Hem or use pinking shears on the top edge, or iron a hem, ½″ or more. Place a few drops of scented oil on the cotton balls, then wrap the cotton with polyester stuffing to keep the oil away from the bag. Stuff the bag and tie it securely with ribbon.

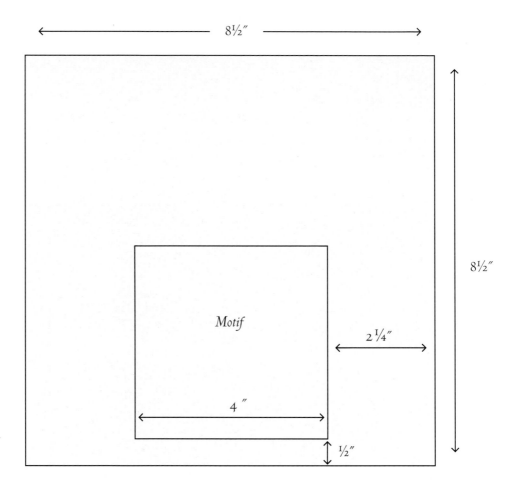

8½″

8½″

Motif

2 ¼″

4 ″

½″

Design layout for sachet bag

FRAMED FLOWERS
LUPINE WITH BUTTERFLY

8" x 10"   *8" x 10"*

Appliqué is like painting with fabric, so why not frame your work of art? You may use glass within your frame, but be sure to mat the piece so the glass does not touch the fabric, as it will draw moisture over time and possibly damage the fabric. Use acid-free mat to prevent yellowing. The design and size possibilities for this project are endless—I have added a small butterfly to the Lupine, which are taller than the basic pattern, to fill the picture. Quilting the piece is optional. Remember, both versions deserve a signature.

MATERIALS (for one picture)
Muslin background and backing: ⅜ yard
Selection of fabrics for appliqué
Matching thread
Dark green and black embroidery floss for details
Batting: 10"x 12" (optional)
Quilting thread (optional)
8" x 10" photo frame

Lupine with butterfly

APPLIQUÉ

Cut one 10″ wide by 12″ high rectangle of background muslin. Appliqué following the numbers. Unnumbered pieces may be added at any time.

EMBROIDERY

Stem stitch the flower stems. Satin stitch the butterfly's body and stem stitch the antennae, finishing with a French knot on the end. Press the finished design after you have removed any markings. Light starch helps stiffen the piece and keeps it from sagging in the frame. If you are not going to quilt the piece it is now ready to frame.

QUILTING

Baste the layers; see page 22. Mark a general 8″ x 10″ perimeter to quilt in. The piece will shrink a bit when quilted, so check now and then as you quilt, as this piece needs to fit in an exact space. If the piece ends up too large you can machine stitch at the 8″ x 10″ line and then trim the edges to fit the frame.

QUILTING DESIGN

Outline the butterfly and echo-quilt around the shape three times, with the lines approximately a ¼″ apart. Mark with masking tape, and using the center of the leaves as a starting point, quilt radiating lines upward toward the butterfly. Fill the rest of the space, from the bottom up, with random shells.

WOODCOCK WITH TRILLIUM
AND VIOLETS

19″ x 16½″

*The Woodcock, often called a Timber Doodle,
can be found on the forest floor in damp and
cool areas. You can hear their peeping, as they
rapidly fly by, as dusk begins with the glow
of the setting sun in spring, summer, and fall.
This is a fun but challenging project.*

MATERIALS

Muslin background and backing: 1 yard
Navy blue inner border: ⅛ yard
Green outer border: ¼ yard
Selection of fabrics for appliqué
Matching thread
Quilting thread in natural color
Green, yellow, white, and brown embroidery floss for details
Batting: 20″ x 17″
Olive green binding: ¼ yard

CUTTING

Muslin background: Cut 16″ x 12½″ rectangle. Trim to 12½″ wide by
10″ high after appliqué and embroidery are complete.
Navy blue inner border: Cut two strips 1½″ wide selvage
to selvage. Measure for exact length before you stitch.
See Borders, page 21.
Green outer border: Cut two strips 2½″ wide selvage to selvage.
Measure for exact length before you stitch. See Borders, page 21.
Olive green binding: Cut two strips 2″ wide selvage to selvage.
Measure for exact length before you stitch. See Binding, page 26.

Woodcock with
Trillium and Violets

Photocopy at 125% to
increase pattern to size
of the finished project

APPLIQUÉ

Appliqué the trillium first. The woodcock will benefit from some pre-appliqué. Follow the numerical sequence indicated on the diagram. Unnumbered pieces may be added at any time.

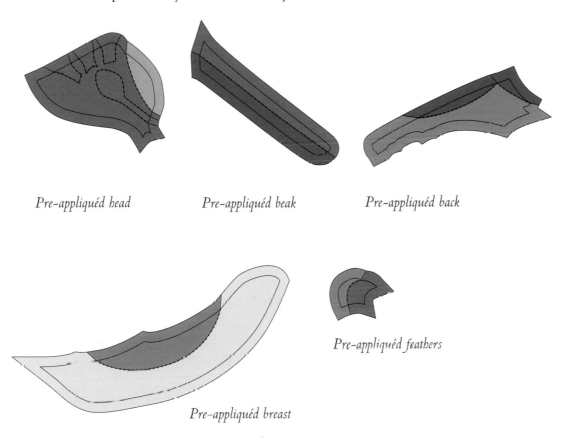

Pre-appliquéd head   *Pre-appliquéd beak*   *Pre-appliquéd back*

Pre-appliquéd feathers

Pre-appliquéd breast

Stitch piece 2 to 1 to form the beak. Stitch pieces 4, 5, 6, 7, and 8 to the head (piece 3). Stitch piece 31 to 30. Take your time with the little pieces, and adjust the size when needed by turning under more or less turn-under allowance. Embroider the details. The eye is a circle of satin stitch in brown, with a ring of white in stem stitch. Add a dot of white to the brown eye for that little gleam! Satin stitch the feet in brown. Remove any markings and press. Trim to 12½" wide by 10" high and add the borders. Press and baste for quilting.

QUILTING

Begin by quilting the sunshine, casting radiating lines on the bird. Start each line at the top, but end them at the inner edge of the first border. Follow with a random pattern of veined leaves scattered about in groups; keep some areas open. Fill in the open areas at the bottom with pebbles. Fill the other areas with random straight lines, marking with masking tape as needed. Check the size; if necessary, trim to return the quilt to square, keeping the borders an even width. Remove the basting, and bind. See Binding, page 26.

WREATH WITH COLORADO COLUMBINE, HARE BELLS, AND VIOLETS

25 ½" x 25 ½"

The wildflower patterns included in this book are adaptable to fit a circular format, as demonstrated in this wreath. The Colorado Columbine, Hare Bells, and Violets were chosen for their varied shapes and compatible colors. Tones of blue and rose highlighted by pure white bring this floral wreath to life. See page 73 for another wreath design idea.

MATERIALS

Muslin background and backing: 1⅔ yards

Dark green border and binding: ⅔ yard

Selection of fabrics for appliqué

Matching thread

Quilting thread in natural color

Medium and dark green, black, and burgundy embroidery floss for details

Batting: 28″ x 28″

CUTTING

Muslin background: Cut a 23″ square; trim to 21″ square after appliqué and embroidery are complete.

Dark green border: Cut three strips 2¾″ wide selvage to selvage. Measure for exact length before you stitch; see Borders, page 21.

Dark green binding: Cut four strips 2″ wide selvage to selvage. Measure for exact length before you stitch; see Binding, page 26.

To create the wreath, use a 16″ circle and the full-size patterns for the Colorado Columbine (page 36), Hare Bell (page 39), and the Violet (page 50). The gridded illustration is provided so that you can gauge the placement of your flowers onto the muslin background. Please note that you will have to slightly change the original patterns to accommodate the circular design.

APPLIQUÉ

Stitch the Columbine stems first using tiny bias strips, see page 17. Then appliqué the remaining flowers following the numerical sequence. Unnumbered pieces may be added any time. Embroider the details, remove any markings, and press. Trim the background to 21″ square, add the borders, and press. Baste for quilting.

QUILTING

First quilt the double line that randomly crosses diagonally across the quilt. Use a string to lay out a nice design and then use a light marker, or your needle, to mark the line. Quilt the double line with ¼″ in between. Add a few random leaflets of three wherever the mood strikes you. Finally, use ¾″ masking tape to mark the diagonal lines, and quilt the design. Start with a line from the upper right to the lower left and quilt to the corners in parallel lines.

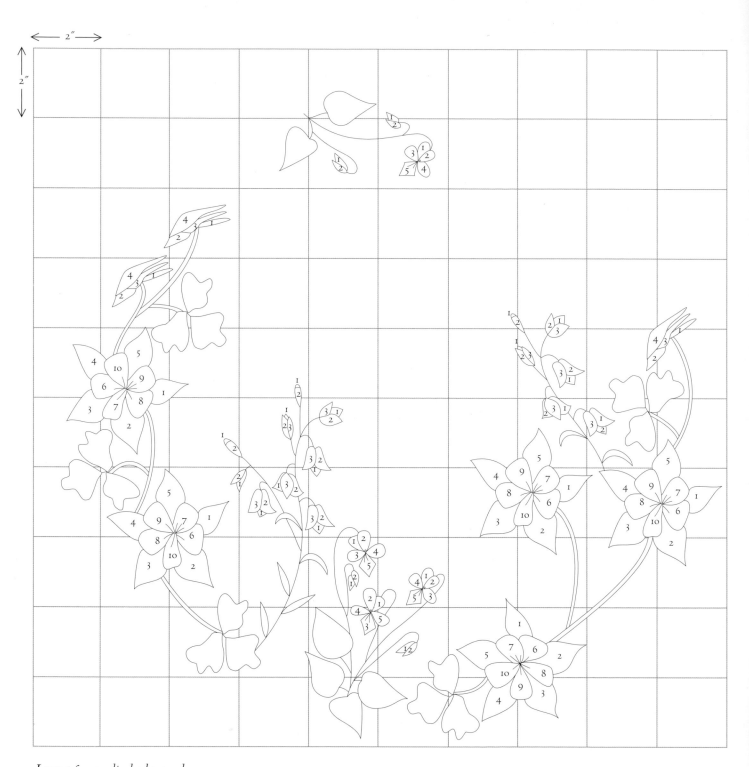

Layout for muslin background

Note: Do not quilt through the double line or the leaflets. Instead, run the needle through the batting layer, then bring the tip up where you want the quilting to continue. Check the size; if necessary, trim to return the quilt to square, keeping the borders an even width. Remove the basting, and bind. See Binding, page 26.

Another wreath design idea

BRIGHT GARDEN

36½" x 25"

Bright Garden is a combination of four designs that are repeated and manipulated to form a line as if they were planted in a garden. The Blue Flag (page 31), the Wood Lily (page 52), Marsh Marigold (page 43), and the Lady's Slipper (page 41) are included. Looking at the wallhanging from left to right, the following changes have been made to the patterns: The stem of the Blue Flag on the left was elongated. The Marsh Marigold and the Wood Lily are unchanged from the pattern on pages 43 and 52. A second Lady's Slipper flower was reversed and added along with one new leaf. The Marsh Marigold on the right was reversed and a flower and leaf were eliminated. The Wood Lily on the right was reversed, the stem was shortened and curved, and a leaf set was eliminated. The Blue Flag on the right has only one flower and one bud. By choosing a combination of bright colors and manipulating the height of the various wildflowers a pleasing design was created from the basic patterns.

MATERIALS
Muslin background and backing: 1½ yards
Red inner border and binding: ⅔ yard
(**Note:** Inner border and binding are the same color)
      Inner border alone: ¼ yard
      Binding alone: ¼ yard

Green outer border: ⅓ yard
Selection of fabrics for appliqué
Matching thread
Quilting thread in natural color
Medium green, light and medium yellow embroidery floss for flower details
Batting: 27″ x 39″

CUTTING

Muslin background: Cut a 33″ wide x 22″ high rectangle. Trim to 31″ wide x 20″ high after appliqué and embroidery are complete.
Red inner border: Cut three strips 1″ wide selvage to selvage. Measure for exact length before you stitch; see Borders, page 21.
Green outer border: Cut three strips 2½″ wide selvage to selvage. Measure for exact length before you stitch; see Borders, page 21.
Red binding: Cut four strips 2″ wide selvage to selvage. Measure for exact length before you stitch; see Binding, page 26.

APPLIQUÉ

Appliqué the flowers in the following order: Lady's Slipper, the Blue Flag on the right, Wood Lilies, Marsh Marigolds, then the Blue Flag on the left. Refer to the numbered wildflower patterns for appliqué order. Any unnumbered pieces may be added at any time. Embroider the details. The tiny bias technique was used for all the stems; see page 17. Remove any markings. Press and trim to 31″ wide x 20″ high. Add the borders and baste for quilting.

QUILTING

Begin by quilting a band of triangles that wave through the center, side to side. Echo the triangles with lines ½″ or so apart, working downward for approximately five inches. Fill in the bottom with pebbles. Quilt random arcs in the top area. Each arc has four lines of quilting ¼″ or so apart. Do not quilt through an already completed arc. Run the needle through the batting layer, bringing the tip up where you want the quilting design to continue. Fill in the spaces created by the arcs with radiating lines going a different direction in each space. These can be marked with ¼″ masking tape. Check the size; if necessary, trim to return the quilt to square, keeping the borders an even width. Remove the basting, and bind. See Binding, page 26.

PASTEL GARDEN

36½" x 25"

Pastel Garden is a collection of seven designs that are repeated and manipulated as in Bright Garden. This group of wildflowers gives a softer look with smaller blooms and cooler colors. The Bloodroot (page 30), Lupine (page 42), Buttercup (page 34), Bunch Berry (page 33), Swamp Rose (page 47), Fireweed (page 37), and Trillium (page 48) are included. Looking at the wallhanging from left to right, the following changes have been made to the patterns: The first Bloodroot is reversed. The Buttercup bud and lower leaf set were eliminated. The Swamp Rose is slightly tilted to the left. The first Fireweed's stem is elongated and five leaves have been added. The right Fireweed's stem is also elongated and one leaf has been eliminated. The Buttercup is tilted slightly to the right. The Bunch Berry, Swamp Rose, and Lupine are reversed. This design cascades from the center Fireweed, with the larger green leaves anchoring the smaller wildflower blooms.

MATERIALS

Muslin background and backing: 1½ yards
Navy blue inner border: ¼ yard
Navy blue binding: ¼ yard
Green outer border: ⅓ yard
Selection of fabrics for appliqué
Matching thread
Quilting thread in natural color
Light, medium, and dark green, and yellow embroidery floss for stems
and flower details
Batting: 27″ x 39″

CUTTING

Muslin background: Cut a 33″ wide x 22″ high rectangle. Trim to 31″
wide x 20″ high after appliqué and embroidery are complete.
Navy blue inner border: Cut three strips 1″ wide selvage to selvage.
Measure for exact length before you stitch; see Borders, page 21.
Green outer border: Cut three strips 2½″ wide selvage to selvage.
Measure for exact length before you stitch; see Borders, page 21.
Navy blue binding: Cut four strips 2″ wide selvage to selvage.
Measure for exact length before you stitch; see Binding, page 26.

APPLIQUÉ

Appliqué the flowers in the following order: Bloodroot, Lupine,
Buttercup, Swamp Rose, Fireweed, Bunch Berry, and finally the Trillium.
Refer to the numbered wildflower patterns for appliqué order. Any
other unnumbered pieces may be added at any time. All the stems are
embroidered with one, two, or three lines of stem stitch, except the
Trillium, which uses the tiny bias technique. The order of the petals on
the Fireweed is not important because they do not overlap. Embroider
the flower details, remove markings, and press. Trim 31″ wide x 20″ high
and add the borders. Baste for quilting.

QUILTING

First, try sketching some small feathers on paper to get an idea of how you want them to look. Then begin with a large feather off-center to the right and a smaller one to the left. Use a string to mark the center vein of the feather. Quilt a double line for the vein with ¼″ space in between. Quilt the feather lines, beginning at the top, working down the sides at the center double line. You will find your feathers are different each time—variation is part of the fun. Surround the feather with teardrops. Using masking tape to mark, and the photo as a reference, radiate lines off to the left and right sides. Then fill in the open center top space with lines radiating from the feather. Fill in the bottom with random shells, starting at the feather and working to both edges. Check the size; if necessary, trim to return the quilt to square, keeping the borders an even width. Remove the basting, and bind. See Binding, page 26.

LILACS

29" x 40"

These are not wildflowers, but most of us are wild about lilacs. You may make a design as large or small as you like by varying the size of the lilacs and background.

MATERIALS

Muslin background and backing: 2½ yards
Selection of fabrics for appliqué: each of the twelve four-petal florets is
a different shade of pink, purple, or blue
Matching thread
Quilting thread in natural color
Black and medium green embroidery floss for the flower centers and stems
Batting: 32″ x 43″
Black binding: ¼ yard

CUTTING

Muslin background: Cut a 32″ wide x 43″ high rectangle. Trim to 29″
wide x 40″ high after appliqué and embroidery are complete.
Black binding: Cut four strips 2″ wide selvage to selvage. Measure for
exact length before you stitch. See Binding, page 26.

APPLIQUÉ

This piece should appear as random blossoms. You may choose to eye
it or, to make it a little simpler, mark a grid of 12″ squares on the background fabric using ¼″ masking tape. It does not need to be perfect.
Refer to the grid diagram for placement and mark the flower placement
using the light box.

 This quilt gives you a lot of freedom in design. Note that each
floret is marked for appliqué order, but not the individual petals. These
can be appliquéd in any order. You may mark the entire flower pattern,
or just mark the centers of each floret and appliqué four petals around
each. The second option gives the flowers a more random look. Either
method will give you wonderful results.

EMBROIDERY

Embroider a double row of stem stitch for the
stems, and stitch French knots for each floret center.
See Embroidery, pages 18-19. Remove any markings
and press. Make sure the piece is reasonably squared.

Full-size Lilac pattern

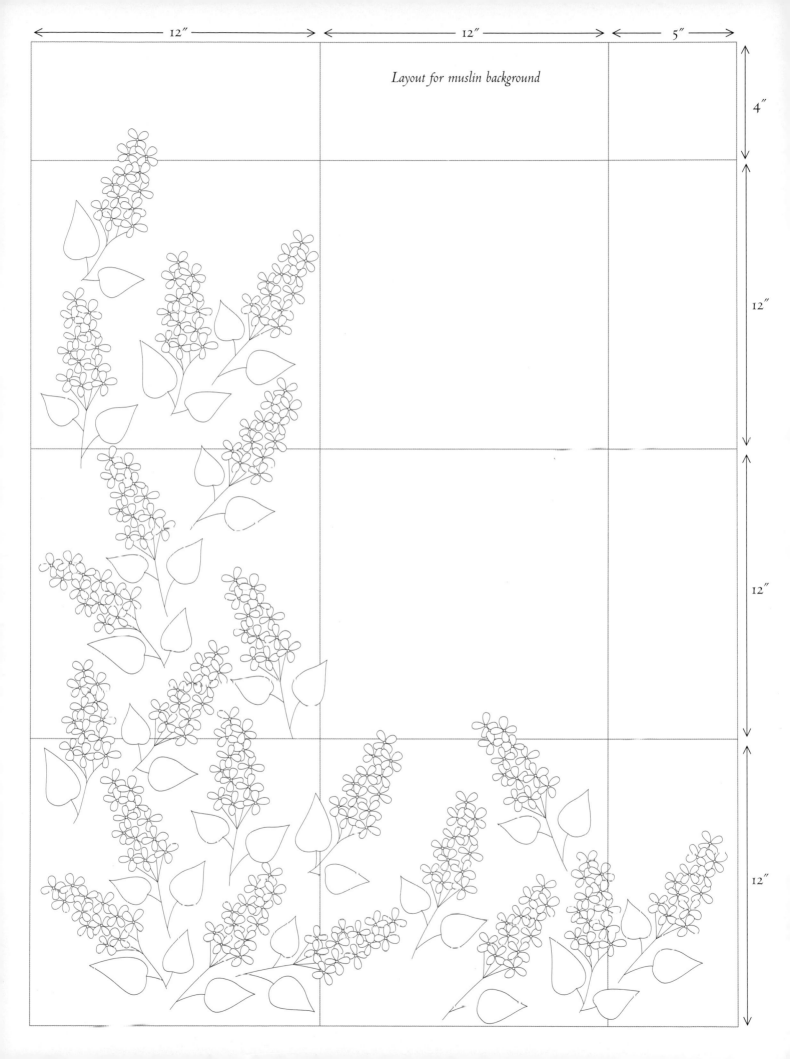

Layout for muslin background

QUILTING

There are two options for marking the tumbling block quilting pattern. The first option is to cut a 2½″ square template from strong paper, stiff interfacing, or a fabric stabilizer. Starting in a corner, pin the 2½″ template to the background. Quilt around the template. Keep moving the template, stitching around it, to form large areas for the parallel lines. Align either by eye or use ¼″ masking tape for marking, and quilt the parallel lines within the squares. Stitch the parallel lines in a different direction within each square. After all of the quilting is complete, check the size; if necessary, trim to return to square. Remove the basting, and bind. See Binding, page 26.

   The second option is to use the pattern on page 85. The pattern repeats top to bottom and side to side. Create a pattern by tracing the solid lines only onto paper. The dotted lines represent quilting that will be added later. Tape the paper pattern onto the light box. Place the background fabric over the paper pattern and trace the solid lines onto the background fabric with a silver or mechanical pencil. Continue tracing to fill the background, moving the fabric around and lining up the solid lines. Quilt the solid lines first, then mark the dotted lines with masking tape and quilt. Stitch the parallel lines in a different direction within each square.

FULL FLOWER FALL

40″ x 42″

This tumble of wildflowers includes one each of the twenty-four wildflower patterns without any changes. It also offers a quilting challenge. You can use all the designs from your quilting library. See pages 24-25.

MATERIALS

Muslin background and backing: 2½ yards
Selection of fabrics for appliqué: a full rainbow of colors
Matching thread
Quilting thread in natural color
Light, medium, and dark green, light and medium yellow, white, and black embroidery floss for stems and wildflower details
Batting: 42″ x 44″
Green binding: ¼ yard

CUTTING:

Muslin background: Cut approximately 42″ x 44″
Green binding: Cut four strips 2″ wide selvage to selvage. Measure for exact length before you stitch; see Binding, page 26.

To create the Full Flower Fall, use all of the full-size patterns for the twenty-four wildflowers (pages 28-52). The gridded illustration is provided so that you can gauge the placement of your flowers onto the muslin background. Please note there are no changes to the original patterns.

APPLIQUÉ

Appliqué each wildflower according to the appliqué order on each pattern. To mark the wildflowers on the background, you may eye the design and mark it as you like, or make a grid using ¼″ masking tape. Mark a 12″ grid on the background fabric. Referring to the grid pattern (page 89), place your wildflowers on the fabric and mark for appliqué. You do not have to be perfect in the placement and can always rearrange the wildflowers to suit your taste. After appliqué and embroidery is complete, remove any markings, and press, making sure the piece is square.

QUILTING

The quilting design consists of 6″ and 8″ squares that randomly tumble across the quilt. Fill each square with any quilting pattern you like. After basting, cut out two paper templates of an 8″ square and a 6″ square. Lay the 8″ template close to the center of the quilt and pin to hold it in place. Using ¼″ masking tape, mark around the outside of the square, then remove the paper; the square is marked and ready to quilt. Quilt on both sides of the ¼″ masking tape for a bold outline. Remove the tape. This is the method you will use to mark all the squares. Only the first square will not have any overlap. Tumble outward from the first square. I used the 8″ template only three times and then used the 6″ template for the rest of the quilt. As you tumble the design, try not to form small squares. Large areas make design placement easier.

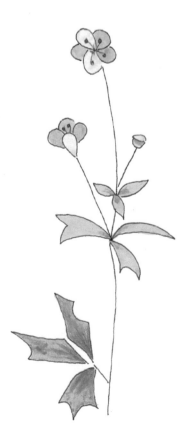

After you have completed a grid of squares, the fun begins. Refer to your quilt library or any quilting books and patterns you like for ideas to fill in the squares. As usual, I used random designs, as they do not require precise markings and give a rich and unique quilting pattern. Check the size; if necessary, trim to return to square, remove the basting, and bind. See Binding, page 26.

Layout for muslin background

DOUBLE WEDDING RING

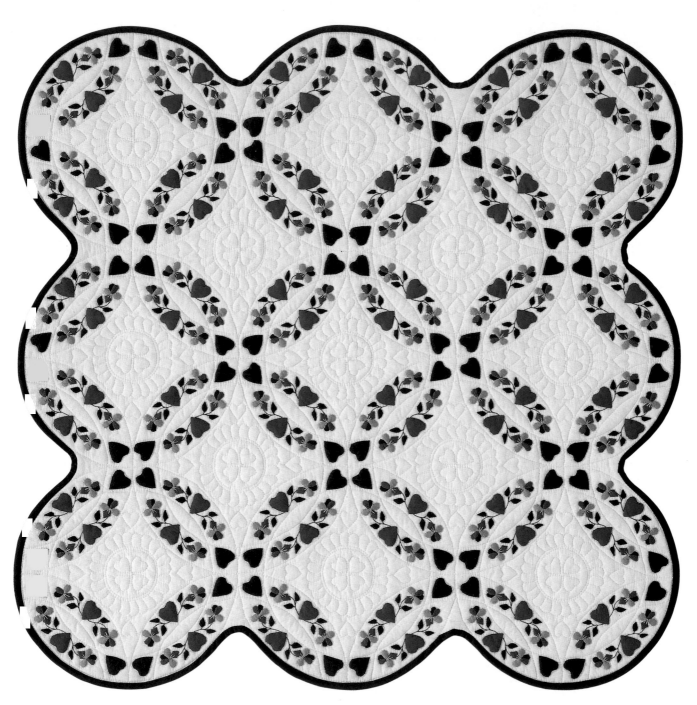

39" x 39"

This quilt adapts the traditional pattern, Double Wedding Ring, for use with wildflower appliqué. The rings are created on a whole piece of fabric which is carefully marked with circles. The repeated flowers and hearts are innovative yet still traditional. Your reward is a beautiful wallhanging.

MATERIALS

Muslin background and backing: 2½ yards
Dark green leaves, hearts, and binding: 1½ yards
Medium green for hearts: ¼ yard
Three shades of pink for the flowers: ¼ yard of each
Matching thread
Quilting thread in natural color
Batting: 42″ x 42″
Dark green, light yellow, and gold metallic embroidery floss for stems and flower details

CUTTING

Muslin background: Cut a 44″ square (to allow yourself room to work.)
Dark green binding: Cut bias strips 2″ wide, selvage to selvage, from the dark green fabric, before cutting the hearts and leaves. You need five yards of bias strips.

CREATING THE GRID

Although you have cut a 44″ square of muslin, the actual pattern is 39″ square. Mark the reference lines for lining up the pattern with a pressing line, then baste both vertically and horizontally. First fold the fabric in half, and press. Mark the fold with a line of basting using a light-colored thread. Carefully measure 13″ from the basted line to the right in several places. Press again or mark lightly and baste the line using a light-colored thread. Repeat for the left side. Refer to the illustration on page 93. Repeat the process for the other direction. Unlike other markings, you can press these without making them permanent.

MARKING THE DESIGN AND APPLIQUÉING

Create a full-circle pattern from the quarter-circle pattern provided. Using the light box, mark the appliqué designs on the fabric. The design is indicated on the pattern by the solid lines; the dotted lines represent the quilting pattern. There are a total of nine circles. Appliqué the design and embroider the details. Remove any markings, but leave the basted reference lines in place. Press.

MARKING THE QUILTING DESIGN

Return the piece to the light box and, using the thread-basted reference lines, mark the quilting design. You may have to ease a line here and there, but small changes will not show in the overall design. Baste the layers for quilting. Quilt following the pattern, then remove the basting.

*One quarter of the Double
Wedding Ring pattern*

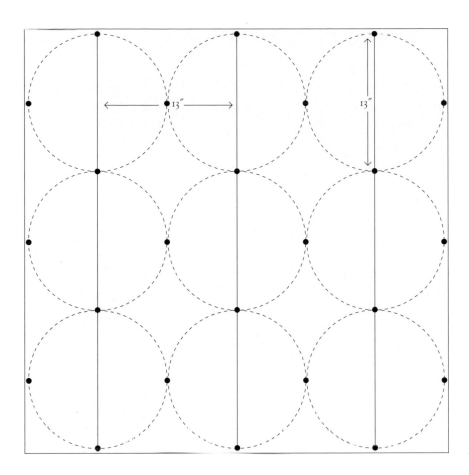

Dot layout

FINISHING

The outer edge of the quilt is trimmed in a gentle curve ½″ from the last quilting line. Also trim a gentle curve where the circles meet. See the illustration below. The binding technique used is a single-fold bias binding that finishes ½″ wide. Join the cut strips to form five yards of bias binding. Pin the binding to the quilt and stitch a ½″ seam on the machine just outside the last line of quilting. Fold and hand stitch the binding to the back with small stitches. Sit back and enjoy your work.

trim line

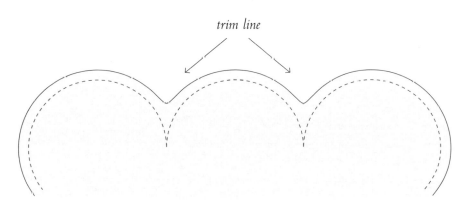

Trim ½″ from the last quilting line

INDEX

ABOUT THE AUTHOR

In 1980 Carol Armstrong taught herself to quilt, developing her unique and highly artistic style where she works mostly with her favorite technique, "Light Box Appliqué." Botanically correct conventionalized celebrations of flora and birds are her strongest output, though any subject that catches her artistic eye may end up a minutely detailed grace on fabric.

Quilting is just one of the many crafts that Carol has tried and mastered purely out of curiosity. As she created her own versions of classic patterns, her mind and fingers explored with the leftover scraps. Quilting quickly grew into an absorption, then her vocation.

In 1986 Carol moved to Michigan's Upper Peninsula, where she lives with her cabinetmaker husband, J.M. Friedrich, in the country near Shingleton. She says the wonderfully snowy winters give her time to do lots of quilting while "Red" makes fine craft items in his workshop a path away. When her fingers and eyes need a break, there is always water to pump and bring in the house, wood to load into the woodbox, bird feeders to fill, or the large organic vegetable garden to tend.

In 1988 Carol published a small line of original quilt patterns and Red followed with the production of beautifully finished, hardwood quilt-thread caddies, adding a pincushion to it. Together they enjoy their creative, homestead lifestyle.

Outdoor photography taken at The Secret Garden Mansion, an elegant Victorian Bed & Breakfast Inn that offers sanctuary among three lovely wooded acres in Walnut Creek, California.
(510) 945-3600

OTHER FINE BOOKS FROM C&T PUBLISHING

For more information write for a free catalog from:
C & T Publishing, Inc.
P.O. BOX 1456
Lafayette, CA 94549
(800) 284-1114
http://www.ctpub.com
e-mail: ctinfo@ctpub.com

For quiltmaking supplies, call or write to:
Cotton Patch Mail Order
3405 Hall Lane, Dept. CTB
Lafayette, CA 94549
e-mail: cottonpa@aol.com
(800) 835-4418
(510) 283-7883